AMY BARTH

101 TIPS

FOR RECOVERING FROM EATING DISORDERS

A POCKET BOOK OF WISDOM

101 Tips for Recovering From Eating Disorders: A Pocket Book of Wisdom
Copyright © 2009 by Amy Barth. All Rights Reserved.
Author info at www.AmyJBarth.com

Library of Congress Cataloging-in-Publication Data

Barth, Amy, 1959-
  101 Tips for recovering from eating disorders : a pocket book of wisdom / by Amy J. Barth.
      p. cm.
  Includes bibliographical references.
  ISBN-13: 978-1-61599-001-6 (trade paper : alk. paper)
  ISBN-10: 1-61599-001-1 (trade paper : alk. paper)
  1. Eating disorders--Popular works. I. Title. II. Title: One hundred one tips for survivors of eating disorders.
  RC552.E18B37 2010
  616.85'26--dc22
                              2009029357

Published by Loving Healing Press
5145 Pontiac Trail
Ann Arbor, MI 48105
Tollfree 888-761-6268
Fax 734-663-6861

www.LovingHealing.com
info@LovingHealing.com

Cover design by Shaila Abdullah

Loving Healing Press

Contents

Dedication

To D.M and her little miracle M.M.,
and
To D.Z: for helping me learn the hard lessons, hanging in there with me through all the ups and downs, knowing when to be "tough" and when to be nurturing... I love you.

Acknowledgments

To my daughters: You are phenomenal—authentic, kind, caring and respectful. As always, so proud of you...

To my publisher, Victor: For keeping at me to get my manuscripts in and being patient when I don't...

Foreword

Congratulations on taking a positive step toward recovery! It took loads of courage to acknowledge old binge, purge, or starve patterns of behavior. Through your journey you will remember your story—who you've been, how you hurt, where you've walked, and what you've done. Every day is a new step in recovery.

Now a new journey begins as you realize your life has more purpose than just to survive. The focus shifts as you determinedly grow more inspired, energized, and fully engaged in your life. In *101 Tips for Recovering from Eating Disorders*, social worker, healer, and compassionate sage Amy Barth provides a goldmine of inspirational tips and ideas to carry you forward into the days ahead.

I always recall a motivational plaque that read, "Life is a do-it-yourself project. Get excited about it!" I love that expression because it reminds us that it's up to us to make each day special. That doesn't mean that each moment of every day is going to be wonderfully smooth, uneventful, and happy. But it does mean that it is our personal responsibility to take action each day to make sure we're excited about being in a body and about being alive. Using tools like the book you are holding now will help you achieve this goal. Use it as a roadmap, a guidebook, and your very own secret path to success.

As you say goodbye and wave farewell to your eating disorder, an opportunity arrives to say hello to moving forward with new understandings. Life is an ever-changing flow of moving, breathing, suffering, and hoping. It includes sorrows and dreams, and the mystery of things actually working out for the best. The transformative powers of your eating disorder journey assist you now in creating a new life experience based on compassion, self-empowerment, worthiness, and trust.

Whenever you're feeling a bit lost, take a few deep slow breaths. Conscious breath instantly lifts your spirits, clears your mind of distressing thoughts, and eases physical tension. Breath is the choice you make to be alive and to be you. Once you've taken a few breaths, open *101 Tips for Recovering from Eating Disorders* and join Amy Barth as she graciously shares her own heart-filled knowledge and insider secrets to creating a rich and satisfying life. Barth's words, culled from years of experience, make this book not only indispensable, but also a roadmap to success.

Dr. Annette Colby
Author, *Your Highest Potentia*

Preface

Eating disorders are formidable foes. I know firsthand. My first encounter was watching my good friend from childhood begin her struggle. It was a struggle that nobody really understood at the time. We were 17 and graduating high school. I went off to college where I too began to struggle. I had a predisposition to developing an eating disorder. I had been sexually abused (85% of girls who are sexually abused develop eating disorders) I was a sensitive kid who strived for perfection.

I had a mother who obsessed about her body and mine. She was always on a diet and she made it clear to me that my body was not OK. I had been a skinny kid but always had a stomach. I still remember my yearly check up at the pediatrician when I was 11, my mother asked the pediatrician, "When will she lose her stomach?" He replied "It's baby fat" and she replied back that "Amy is 11 years old and this is definitely not baby fat." She gave me a very loud and clear message that my body was not OK. The same year, my brother-in-law gave me the nick name 'ST' (for spare tire) he still calls me that to this day... The message was clear from all of them, *my body was not OK.*

When I was 15, my mother wanted to send me to "fat camp" for the summer even though I was within the normal weight range. There it was, another message that my body was not OK. At 16, I joined Weight Watchers® and followed the diet to a "T"! (striving for perfection). I don't remember if I actually lost any weight, but it made my mom happy! My mom was petite and my older sister is petite and I always felt like the "Jolly Green Giant" next to them.

My freshman year, I discovered Feen-a-Mint (the laxative Bisacodyl) along with my dorm-mates. They chewed the chalky gum occasionally, but my habit developed into a full blown eating disorder. I struggled with it on and off in college. My senior year, I lost a lot of weight and my mother rewarded me with a shopping spree. She was so happy, I was finally a size 5. I wonder if she would have been so happy if she knew how I achieved those results? Actually it was quite miserable, though in the late 1970s and into the early 80s, nobody recognized what I was doing. It was never addressed. Fast forward to age 22, my fiancé told me to choose between him and my laxatives... I chose him and was in recovery from my eating disorder for the next 21 years. I was busy raising my family and was very conscious not to expose my daughters to any of this....

In 2003, I started my healing from Childhood Sexual Abuse and my eating disorder returned with a vengeance. I had to numb those painful feelings and what better way, then engaging in disordered eating? For four months, I descended into "eating disorder hell" As I started to heal, I started to give up my disordered eating. I would go months and then have a couple of days lapse and it went on for several years until *I finally recovered!* Eating disorders are not about food, they are dangerous and they are always a symptom of an underlying issue....

If you are struggling, please use the tips in this book to help you on the slippery slope to recovery. Recovery is liberating. You won't regret it. I am so proud of you for beginning down this road.. I know you can do it...Good luck!

Amy Barth,
August 2009

1. There are no perfect people (to stop striving for perfection, it doesn't exist).

2. To find my authentic self (done).

3. To accept and love my apple shaped body. (Thin limbs and a round middle) yup, that's me!

4. Not to care what other people say about me, it's none of my business (I admit this is hard).

5. Not to listen when people talk about the diets they are on (diets don't work).

6. To eat when I am hungry and stop when I am satisfied.

7. I can eat anything in moderation.

8. To move my body.

9. To stop weighing myself and throw away the scale.

10. That it is ok to ask for what you need.

AND

I am just wonderfully me!

How to Use this Book

- Highlight the tips that resonate with you, so that you can find them quickly, when you need them.

- Please make this your mantra and say it everyday: "I can recover."

- You can turn any tip into an affirmation. An affirmation is a declaration that something is true. Affirmations should avoid negations such as "don't" or "not". Rewrite them in positive language only.

- Post affirmations on your mirror, in your locker, in any private space that is your own.

- Sometimes a tip will bring up resistance, emotions, or unexplained tears. Try journaling about your feelings and reactions when embracing a challenging tip.

What an eating disorder is and is *not*

1. Eating disorders are a serious psychological illness that combine social and biological factors.

2. Eating disorders are a symptom of an underlying issue.

3. Eating disorders are insidious.

4. Eating disorders are self-destructive.

5. Eating disorders can kill you.

6. Eating disorders are *not* about food.

7. You deserve to eat, it's a basic need.

8. Every body needs nourishment.

9. There are no bad foods, you can eat everything in moderation.

10. Eat when you are hungry and stop when you are satisfied.

11. Don't use food to cope with your feelings, that includes: starving, overeating, binging and purging, chewing and spitting, or taking laxatives.

12. You will have intrusive thoughts and you will have to fight the voice in your head.

13. It is hard to quiet the thoughts in your head on your own.

14. Don't give power to the voice in your head, don't engage in eating disordered behavior.

15. Fight the voice in your head that tells you to binge and purge, starve, take laxatives, or exercise obsessively.

16. Ignore the voice in your head that tells you that you have to be perfect.

17. Ignore the voice that tells you, you are a failure (that voice is wrong)

18. Eating disorders usually require professional help (Very few people can do it alone).

19. There is no shame in asking for help.

20. It is a sign of strength to ask for help when you need it.

21. Find a therapist you like
(you have to click or it won't help).

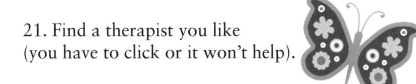

22. Try different types of therapy: art, music, drama, movement, ropes, pet, equine, dolphin, photography, journaling, EFT...

23. Join a support group (there are many out there).

24. Find a nutritionist that can help you make good decisions about food.

25. Recognize that when you are "in" your eating disorder, that you are not a good judge of how you look. (Believe what your helping professional is saying about that area of your life).

26. Be open to processing new ways to see things.

27. Be relentless in figuring out what the underlying issue is (trust your helping professional).

28. Allow people to take care of you.

29. Feelings aren't right or wrong. They just are...

30. It's OK to be angry, sad, scared, anxious, _____. (Fill in the blank)

31. It's OK to cry and it can be cleansing

32. You may have suicidal thoughts (if you feel this way, please talk to someone, call a hotline or go to your nearest emergency room).
Do not act on the thoughts!

33. Find healthy ways to cope with feelings: go for a walk, journal, call or e-mail a friend, write a letter, paint, draw, knit, write poetry or a story, collage, doodle, color, crochet, do a puzzle, laugh, meditate, breathe... (add to this list!)

34. Stop weighing yourself!

35. Remember as long as you are healthy, your weight does not matter, it is just a number on the scale.

36. Smash the scale!

37. Don't *ever* buy another scale.

38. Ask yourself whether the sensation is Emotional or Physical.

39. Eat *only* when you are physically hungry.

40. Become aware of your body's signals.

41. You deserve to be healthy and happy.

42. Take 10 deep cleansing breaths when you are having a rough moment.

43. Learn to soothe yourself.

44. Nurture yourself.

45. Have compassion for yourself.

46. Have patience with yourself.

47. Ask for what you need.

48. Connect with others.

49. Listen to your inner voice.

50. Adopt healthy coping mechanisms.

51. Speak up for yourself, your opinion counts.

52. Find ways to build your self esteem (make a list of all the things you are good at).

53. Post the list on your bathroom mirror, on the dash of your car, in your locker.

54. Find friends who accept you for who you are.

55. Don't hang around with people who judge other people by their weight, looks etc. (it's what is inside that counts).

56. Stop punishing yourself.

57. Remember you are not alone.

58. Nobody expects you to be perfect
(there are no perfect people).

59. Do yoga and meditate.

60. Be yourself!

61. Don't compare yourself to anybody else.
You are a wonderful and unique individual.

62. Read (there is a wealth of info out there.)

63. Respect your body for what it does for you.

64. Your body is the vessel for your soul.

65. Write a love letter to your body and note all the things you love about your body.

66. Stop saying negative things about your body, ie: my stomach is too fat, my thighs are too big (you get the idea).

67. Do not compare yourself with models or other media images (They are airbrushed).

68. Start each day by looking in the mirror and saying something nice about your body(Do it until it becomes a habit).

69. Listen to what your body needs.

70. Live in your body, Love it, Respect it, Move it.

71.You can fully recover.

72. Take it slow.

73. It will take time.

74. Have patience with yourself.

75. It takes strength to recover from an eating disorder.

76. Stay focused.

77. Be mindful.

78. It is very tough, but hang in there.

79. Set realistic expectations for yourself.

80. Be open to new experiences.

81. Fight to get better.

82. Recovery may be the hardest fight of your life.

83. You may lapse after a period of recovery and you will have to pick yourself up and start again.

84. Don't ever give up on yourself.

85. You have unlimited potential, you can fight this and you can win!

86. Volunteer with groups that are working to create awareness and prevent eating disorders.

87. Imagine how wonderful life would be if you were free of your eating disorder.

88. Wear a rubber band or a bracelet for every day you go without engaging in your eating disorder (when you get to 30 days, treat yourself to a manicure, a movie or anything that feels like a reward)

89. Do that for every month you get through without engaging in your eating disorder.

90. Fill a box with things you can do when you are having a rough time(a funny movie, crossword puzzles, crafts, phone numbers for friends). Please add to this list.

91. Believe in yourself and make it your mantra until you believe it, *I will recover, I will recover...*
I know you will!

92. You are loved.

93. You have value.

94 .You matter.

95. You are special.

96. Be true to yourself.

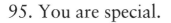

97. Believe in yourself, you can do this.

98. There is hope.

99. Carpe Diem (Seize the day).

100. Life is a gift.

101. Remember, you can recover! Make it your mantra and say it everyday until you believe it: *I will recover, I will recover...*

10 Things to do when having a rough time

- Take ten deep cleansing breaths
- Listen to a guided imagery CD
- Call, e-mail or write a letter to a friend
- Watch your favorite comedy
- Take a bubble bath
- Scream
- Dance
- Laugh
- Sing
- Make a list of what you are grateful for

1. Journal about what the voice of your eating disorder is saying to you .

2. Do a collage that represents your feelings.

3. Do a collage of your needs and then start voicing what you need to others.

3. Make a deck of cards or a collage of the strong people in your life that you can reach out to during difficult times.

4. Draw a picture of how you think you look and then ask somebody else to draw a picture of you. Compare the pictures.

5. Keep a gratitude journal.

6. Say *one* nice thing about yourself everyday and keep a running list.

7. Burn a CD of music you like.

8. It takes strength to recover from an eating disorder. What does strength mean to *you*? Try different forms of art to express strength.

9. Design a t-shirt about recovering from an eating disorder. Wear it during National Eating Disorder Awareness Week in February.

10. Express in as many ways as you can what recovery looks like to you.

11. Write your own book about tips for recovery...

Schaefer, J., & Rutledge, T. (2004). *Life without Ed How one woman declared independence from her eating disorder and how you can too.* New York: McGraw-Hill.

From the Introduction: "Ed and I lived together for more than twenty years. He was abusive, controlling, and never hesitated to tell me what he thought, how I was doing it wrong, and what I should be doing instead... Ed is not a high school sweetheart. Ed is not some creep that I started dating in college... Ed's name comes from the initials E.D. —as in eating disorder. Ed is my eating disorder."

Johnston, A. A. (2000). *Eating in the light of the moon: How women can transform their relationships with food through myths, metaphors & storytelling.* Carlsbad, Calif: Gúrze Books.

Written in a readable and intimate style, each of the twenty chapters explores a different theme of empowerment and self-discovery. A great gift for someone in recovery!

In addition to being immensely enjoyable reading, Eating in the Light of the Moon is filled with practical exercises and profound insights. Twenty chapters explore different themes of self-discovery and empowerment on core issues such as:

Intuition: The Inner Seeing, Hearing, Knowing
Symbolism: Hunger as a Metaphor
Feelings: Gifts from the Heart
Moontime: Reclaiming the Body's Wisdom
Dreamtime: The Journey Within
Sexuality: Embracing the Feminine
Recovery: Out of the Labyrinth

About the Author

Amy Barth is a thriver possessing a passion for girls and women who need to be set free in their mind and their hearts. Because of her extensive background in social work, she founded the nonprofit Safe Girls Strong Girls in 2005. SGSG is committed to breaking the silence of Childhood Sexual Abuse (CSA) and is giving girls their voices back. One project of SGSG is Camp CADI, a one-of-a-kind week long camp where girls learn how to heal and just be girls again. Please visit **www.SafeGirlsStrongGirls.org**

Amy is the author of several books including *Will the Courageous, Annabelle's Secret, 101 Tips for Survivors of Sexual Abuse: A Pocket Book of Wisdom*. Amy lives near Atlanta, Georgia with her husband Paul and their college-age daughters.

Amy's website is **www.AmyJBarth.com**

Other Great Books for Survivors
from Loving Healing Press

AM I BAD?

Recovering from Abuse

HEYWARD BRUCE EWART, III, PhD

REPAIR
YOUR LIFE

A Program for Recovery from
Incest & Childhood Sexual Abuse

Marjorie McKinnon

got parts?

An INSIDER'S GUIDE
to MANAGING LIFE
SUCCESSFULLY
with DISSOCIATIVE
IDENTITY DISORDER

by ATW

Gifts From
The Child Within
Second Edition

Barbara Sinor, PhD

LaVergne, TN USA
04 June 2010
184991LV00001B